Augustine Uteno Obaje

Being and Sexuality: A Cultural Reflect of African Modern Christians

Augustine Uteno Obaje

Being and Sexuality: A Cultural Reflect of African Modern Christians

This is a study about Africentric sexuality. Thus, the study examines the Christian concepts of sexuality in Africa

Blessed Hope Publishing

Imprint
Any brand names and product names mentioned in this book are subject to trademark, brand or patent protection and are trademarks or registered trademarks of their respective holders. The use of brand names, product names, common names, trade names, product descriptions etc. even without a particular marking in this work is in no way to be construed to mean that such names may be regarded as unrestricted in respect of trademark and brand protection legislation and could thus be used by anyone.

Cover image: www.ingimage.com

Publisher:
Blessed Hope Publishing
is a trademark of
Dodo Books Indian Ocean Ltd. and OmniScriptum S.R.L publishing group

120 High Road, East Finchley, London, N2 9ED, United Kingdom
Str. Armeneasca 28/1, office 1, Chisinau MD-2012, Republic of Moldova, Europe
Printed at: see last page
ISBN: 978-620-4-18831-7

Acknowledgements

I acknowledge God for giving me the wisdom and grace to complete this study. I am indebted to my supervisor, Dr. Katrina A. Korb for guiding me through the writing of this research. I thank Professor Theresa Adamu for always encouraging me to push on in the name of Jesus. Also to professor Joel K.T. Biwul, who relentlessly taught me communicating skills which have greatly assisted in this work. To Pastor Emmanuel Kure at the Library and Pastor Kingsley K. Onuoha, for taking me through research and writing.

I am eternally grateful to my wife (my heart) Sarah Augustine Obaje and all our children: Jill, Jemaimah, and Bethany who prayed and supported daddy in the process of the thesis. My wife and friend, you have continued to remain a virtuous woman despite the various storms that came our way in order to stop the school. She supported me so much in all areas; she is blessed of the Lord. I thank my children for their patience throughout the studies.

My profound gratitude goes to my faculty adviser, Prof. Yusufu Turaki. May God bless you sir. My special thanks to the entire JETS community, faculty and staff for being part of my life at JETS. What could I have achieved without my class and school mates motivation, I thank you all. I appreciate the Byang Kato Liberians for making available books and facilities used for the research.

TABLE OF CONTENTS

CHAPTER   PAGE

I.   INTRODUCTION...4

          Background of the Study

          Statement of Problem

          Purpose of the Study

          Significance of the Problem

          Definition of Terms

          Research Questions

          Delimitation of the Study

          Summary

II.   LITERATURE REVIEW...25

          Introduction
          Overview of Sex Education
          Origin of Sexuality Education
          Abstinence Sex Education
          HIV/AIDS Sexual Education Program
          Biblical Basis for Sex Education
          Summary

III RESEARCH METHODOLOGY.. 40

    Research Design

    Participants

    Instrument

    Procedure for Data Collection

    Data Analysis

IV. DATA PRESENTATION AND ANALYSIS..................................... 56

    Introduction

    Data Presentation, Analysis and Interpretation

V. DISCUSSION, RECOMMENDATIONS AND CONCLUSION................. 65

    Discussion

    Recommendations

    Conclusion

Abstract

This is an anthropo-theological study of sexuality among modern African Christians. Thus, the study examines the concept of sexuality among modern African Christians by seeking to extend the frontiers of knowledge on the topic. It is observed that African Christians carry two identities; Christianity and traditional culture-bearer. These have far-reaching effects on the people socially and religiously as the two have in it, the concept of moral rules. Data indicate that African societies, at various points, construe sexual relationship as a sacrosanct factor in their image of an ideal society, and a respectable phenomenon, which every member of the society must adhere to the rules guiding it. The study notes that on one hand, modern African Christians are faced with the challenge of expressing sexuality and its different colorations within the confine of Judeo-Western Christianity bequeathed to them by Western missionaries, and on the other hand, they are confronted with expression of sexuality within their traditional cultural norms. Methodologically, the study uses documented ethnographic data from anthropological studies of some notable African societies and biblical exegesis. It is clear from the study that in Africa, sexuality is attached with high level of sacredness, especially in traditional communities, which have come under heavy doses of westernization, *sinoization* (Chinese influence) and globalization. Findings show that Christians in Africa are dissected and torn between two worlds of Westernized Christianity and traditional African culture, out of which they are forced to forge a new identity.

Keywords: Africans, Anthropo-theology, Christians, Sexuality, Traditional societies

Introduction

Our knowledge of human sexuality can be enhanced by intermix of anthropology and theology because human beings are sexual beings and religion impinges on their sexual activities. The paper is exploratory and discursive, as it seeks to extend the frontiers of discourse of anthropology and theology on human sexuality by focusing on modern African Christians. The interconnectivity of anthropology and theology is capable of making meaningful contributions to the discourse on humanity and its beliefs. Scholars like Davies Douglas (2002) and Robins (2006) have highlighted the relevance of such studies. It is germane in this study because human sexuality portends great discussion for scholars on African culture, African Christians and Christianity in general. The study notes that African Christians are invariably torn between competing interests on human intersexuality both traditional and modern that impose severe demands on them, which are more pronounced among modern African Christians. They are confronted with ideologies/philosophies and existential realities such as homosexuality, gay/lesbianism and transgender issues on one hand versus their deeply rooted traditional ethos on the other hand. They are also contending with variants of biblical perspectives, westernization and globalization, which are currently exerting great influence on them. In addition, there are unending buffeting with media onslaughts, which present conflicting ideas on sexuality among Africans.

The study observes that the concept of sexuality is losing its traditional normative meaning among Africans in general, a fact, which affects African Christians. In this light, Alimi,(2015) a well-known Nigerian gay and gay activist asserts, "If you say being gay is not African, you don't know your history". To show the "unAfricanness" of gay/lesbianism, some African countries have criminalized same sex relations. This forces Arimoro (2018) to ask, if criminalization of same-sex relations is a protection of African culture? It is therefore, imperative to examine the unfolding sense of sexuality and ultimately male and female relationships within Africans who profess Christianity. Viewing from all angles in this paper, the origin and development of humanity, one thing had remained constant in all, sex and sexual relationships remain the core of which the reproduction of human beings rest.

The focus on African Christians is justifiable because, they form a sizable population of the world. Africa is home to the largest Christian population numbering circa 685 million. It is estimated that by 2025, there will be 760 million Christians in Africa, according to projections of the World Book encyclopedia. Christianity has many faces in the continent, a fact derived from healthy syncretistic modus operandi of African religionists. Scholars state that there are extensive syncretic tendencies in African religions in general. According to Mbiti (1992: 15), this is a blessing indeed, as "when Africans have converted to other religions, they often mix their traditional religion with the one to which they are converted. In this way they are not losing something valuable, but are gaining something from both religions". And according to Riggs (2006:1), although a large proportion of Africans have converted to Islam and Christianity, these two worlds have been enculturated by Africans to suit their preferences and traditional orientations.

The study uses written ethnographic data collected in some African cultural settings and biblical exegesis. The paper explores the opinions, attitudes and discernible practices among modern African Christians on human sexuality. To bring the study into proper perspectives, the paper discusses the traditional tenets of human sexuality within Africa and notes that these tenets have come under deep pressure from foreign religions and modern media. The study notes that what might be the pristine believe of Africans about human sexuality has been largely subsumed under Islam and Christianity and heavily influenced by modern media.

Teenagers these days seem to be neglected in many homes in terms of sex education. Biblical principles teach the fact that teenagers are also created by God. They need the involvement of parents in their teenage years. Indeed, preparing them for transition to adulthood has always been one of humanity's great challenges. Today, in a world with AIDS, how parents meet its challenge is a deliberate venture and an important opportunity to breaking the trajectory of the epidemic. Teenagers receive arrange of inaccurate messages about sexuality almost on a daily basis. It is hoped that a close parental based involvement on sexuality education can help teenager navigate the unchristian messages. In some Nigerian communities today, there are some teenagers who are practically growing without parental involvement. It therefore brings to mind that the need for parents to be involved and teach sexuality education in Nigerian society and beyond cannot be overemphasized. There are considerable cultural and value differences between different religions and tribes that seem to have affected parental involvements in sex education. Teenagers seem to be asking so many questions about sexuality that might not be answered by parents unless they are involved in their lives. John White talking to parents puts it that, "Children came into the world as tabula rasa-clean slate for parents to write on"(White,1979:22).

Background of the Study

Teenagers these days seem to be neglected in many homes in terms of sex education. Biblical principles teach the fact that teenagers are also created by God. They need the involvement of parents in their teenage years. Indeed, preparing them for transition to adulthood has always been one of humanity's great challenges. Today, in a world with AIDS, how parents meet its challenge is a deliberate venture and an important opportunity to breaking the trajectory of the epidemic. Teenagers receive a range of inaccurate messages about sexuality almost on a daily basis. It is hoped that a close parental based involvement on sexuality education can help teenagers navigate these unchristian messages. In some Nigerian communities today, there are some teenagers who are practically growing without parental involvement. It therefore brings to mind that the need for parents to be involved and teach sexuality education in Nigerian society and beyond cannot be overemphasized. There are considerable cultural and value differences between different religions and tribes that seem to have affected parental involvements in sex education. Teenagers seem to be asking so many questions about sexuality that might not be answered by parents unless they are involved in their lives. John White talking to parents puts it that, "Children came into the world as tabula rasa-clean slate for parents to write on" (White, 1979:22).

Parental Communication

Should parents shy away from giving sexual guidance and knowledge to their teenagers? The bible admonishes parents to get involved in teaching children and teenagers about God's and His ways. Proverbs 22:6 encourages parents to train their children in the way he should go and when he is old he will not turn from it. This is to say parents are also to get involved in the sexual education of their teenagers so that when they are grown they will be able to choose the right path and remain in it like Joseph in the house of Potipher. Sexuality communication with teens can go a long way to help them develop personal values and be able to make good moral decisions in life. The fact remains, God is the perfect parent. The way He relates to us and wants us to grow to maturity is an example of how parents should relate to their teenagers to grow and mature. The bible puts it to say, "Lo children are a heritage of the Lord: and the fruit of the womb is his reward" (Ps 127:3, KJV). The teenagers are gifts to their parents from God and they bring great joy and benefit when they are correctly communicated to in matters of sexuality. They can on the other hand bring challenges and stresses to parents if they are not well brought up.

Parents who love their children ought to determine to teach them sexual education before others give them their own ideas about it. Sexuality, apart from its reproductive function ought to play the role of uniting a man and a woman in terms of intimacy that cannot be achieved in any other way (Morakinyo, 2002: 23). If it is badly used, sex can cause overwhelming physical and moral problems. Ideal parenting should be involving and interactive between parents and teens day in and day out (Balswick, 1992:93). It is therefore important that responsible parents educate their teenagers on issues of sex. The goal therefore, is to instruct teens on how to engage in sexual activity while avoiding pitfalls such as unwanted pregnancies or sexually transmitted diseases, explaining that God designed the man and woman to be sexual beings so that they can enjoy their sex with responsibility.

From the early age, teens can be taught physical education, vocational training, religious education, and respect for elders so as to form responsible character in the society. The absence of any of any other aspect of education is tolerable as long as sexual education is not left out. The implication of the absence of sexuality education is the most shameful thing that a teen can inflict on his or her families members (Fafunwa, 2004:12).

Sex related information is everywhere now, especially on television, handset, and billboards. In a typical traditional setting like that of Kishika community, cultural practices often prevent some of the parents from giving prompt sexuality knowledge to teenagers. In as much as contemporary parents in homes might have differing views as a result of cultural differences in passing across sexuality education, it becomes necessary to mention that the home is the very foundation where sex education should begin. Parents are to understand that God will hold them responsible for communicating their teenagers in all aspects of life. Just as God communicates through the Scriptures, so parents should follow his example in educating their teens. This is how the Bible puts it:

> And you must commit yourselves wholeheartedly to these commands that I am giving you today. Repeat them again and again to your children. Talk about them when you are at home and when you are on the road, when you are going to the bed and when you are getting up. Tie them to your hands and

wear them on your forehead as reminders. Write them on the doorposts of your house and on your gates (Deut 6:6-9 NLT).

Apart from God's plan, teenagers need the active involvement of both father and mother for godly behaviour to be developed in them. Indeed, parents are called to be their teenagers' primary educators.

Cultural Taboos in the Discussion of Sexuality

Many cultures have taboos on the discussion of sex issues especially in the Nigerian society. Ordinarily, whenever sex is mentioned, people tend to show a refrained action. It is often seen as a cultural, social and religious taboo especially when it is coming out from the mouth of a teenager. In Africa, sex knowledge is usually very difficult to impart from parent to children (Mbiti, 1989:132). It is certainly not easy to talk on sexuality. This is probably because it is not customary to do so. A typical African parent might never be seen talking about sex related issues with their children. As far as some of them are concerned, sex discussion is a realm considered completely a taboo. This is rightly observed by Danfulani Kore when he said "communication between parents and children is generally poor because in many cultures, children do not sit together with their parents, especially their fathers…..children are left on their own until the time they get married" (Kore, 2012:79). This is probably the reason some of the parents who adhere to cultural taboos fear that telling their teens about sex will spoil them. The traditional Hausa parents seem to be concern that differing sexual values and customs will corrupt their children. Just as it is being observed by the researcher in northern Nigeria where there is the culture of parental persuasion on teenagers especially females, the parents basically decides who, how and when the daughters will get married by cultural practice. The parents therefore assumed it is unnecessary to discuss sexuality with young people. For the Yoruba's, sexuality is a core matter of human life hence Olugboyega Alaba buttress to say:

> Sexual intercourse and the methods of doing it is not discussed openly with children but taught to them cautiously at the appropriate time, in closed groups. Married couples also discuss and express it purposefully for procreation, mainly. Anxiety is not encouraged at all in this regard. That is why a bridegroom is usually politely kept out of the house while his newly bride is being brought in. He will then be brought in to meet his wife after the ritual washing of her feet has been done (Alaba, 2004: 11).

This is to say there is a gap between parents and teenagers in terms of interaction on sexual matter which represent an important part of the teenager's life and future. This culture then holds that the appropriate time for sexual education is when one is married. This posse a big challenge in today's age when media is exposing teenagers to issues of sexuality at an early age. Some parents sometimes think that exposing teenagers to learn about sexuality could make them want to get practically experiment sex which may lead to pregnancy or sexually transmitted disease. Such pregnancy and STDs could be avoided if sex education was taught earlier in the homes. If parents who are custodians of culture were involved it would have also helped the teenagers to know more about the biological development of their bodies. It is said that it is possible that Primary school boys and girls are already engaged in sex and they are likely to continue to engage in premarital sex with or without sex education (Ndiragu, 2000:68).

Religiously, the African traditional religious cultures also prohibits discussions of sexuality before teenagers, it is regarded a taboo for young people to listen or receive such information before they are married. Akintunde Olu and Ayantayo K. expressed that "Sex is considered sacred in all its forms and interpretation. And as a matter of fact, it is something that must not be talked about. "Anything that relates to romance and sex is done secretly" (Akintunde and Ayantayo, 2005: 4). The question then is how teenagers can know anything about sexuality when their own parents may refuse to talk about it probably because of cultural traditions. The teenagers are held in darkness for lack of orientation unless they get to see or hear from media sources which might not be the best of options. Again, some in Islam and other denominations under the umbrella of Christianity have not help matters as they also assumed the culture of no need to talk about sexuality with young people. It is said:

The Islamic injunction believes that both the Islamic moral philosophy and the social system of Islam have adequately taken care of the sexual problems beyond the conception and scope of sexuality education. It is strongly believed that religious knowledge, be it Islam or Christianity helps children to cultivate religious attitude towards life and orientate them towards self purification, self actualization and socialization. Both Christianity and Islam do not see the need for sexuality education in Nigeria (Adunola, 2005:11).

Importance of Discussing Sexuality

Against the popular prevailing culture of unchristian and inaccurate media messages on social media like facebook, twitter, among others has made it very pertinent to charge parents towards discussing sexuality with their teens at home. Oyenike A. Oyinloye thinks it is important to discuss sex education with young people through parents as she says "sexuality education acquaints the youth with factual and accurate sexual information about the dimension of sexual knowledge that will enable them understand and clarify their personal values and improve their knowledge which will in turn assist them in sexual decision making" (Oyenike, 2014:2). This then confers on the teen a sense of sexual responsibility, and then builds in him or her moral confidence with understanding of what sex is all about. He or she can then use the understanding as a weapon to fight against ignorance in the mist of unchristian sex messages in media today.

Statement of Problem

Teenage Pregnancy

Sexual misbehaviours and unintended pregnancy among teenagers is gradually growing and becoming a universal problem. A recent report by Adogu and colleagues in International Journal of Clinical Medicine states that:

> About 16 million teenagers 15-19 years old give birth each year, contributing to 11% of all births worldwide. Seventy percent of all adolescents' birth takes place in sub-Saharan Africa. In Nigeria, by the age of 19 years, 23% of teens must have given birth to a child. In further studies carried out among female adolescents in Port Harcourt which reported 78.8% prevalence, Owerri which gave a prevalence of 31.6% with 78.9% pregnancy recurrence (Adogu, 2014:2).

In Kishika district, Bassa L.G.A Plateau State, teenage sex is not encouraged culturally. The culture is in support of sanctity of sexuality but with the waves of the new age, the aspect of sanctity is gradually giving way. The researcher recently noticed that there is increase in the rate of which teenagers especially girls drop out of schools because of untimely pregnancy. A recent visit to Kishika for preliminary survey reveals that pregnancy among very young adolescents is a major problem.

Among 13 families that were visited in their homes, 8 teens within the range of 15-16 years were already pregnant. Three parents were already asking the young ladies with their babies to join the boys that impregnated them. A privileged information from one of the teenage mothers said there was one day she asked the mother what sex was all about, but the mother could not answer her. She rather responded with a question saying "why do you ask about sex, where did you hear it, and what do you want to do with it? When I was your age I never imagine sex talk less of vomiting the nonsense out of my mouth". According to the unfortunate teenage mother, she could only imagine sex but never talk about it after that incidence. Being a JSS1 Student, one day she asked her male English teacher what sex was all about, the teacher took advantage of the opportunity and asked her to come to the house for the lecture and she did, it was more of practical. That was how the young girl became pregnant and had to stop school.

Teenage Pregnancy and Abortion

Teenage pregnancy and abortion is often associated with premarital sex. When a pregnancy is an outcome of premarital sex, most teenagers resort to abortion as a way of concealing their acts in order to avoid embarrassments. The girl feels ashamed to carry a pregnancy that is out of wedlock while the boy responsible for the pregnancy is not mature enough to tackle the responsibilities of fatherhood.

According to C.C. Dike:

> The act of pregnancy is often commonly associated with females while males co-pilot the affair. An unsuccessful abortion could lead to death or the destruction of the womb. It could also lead to childlessness at later years. On the other hand, if the girl decides to carry the pregnancy to term, she may experience difficulty in delivering the baby. Labor may be obstructed and the baby and mother may die (Dike, 2000:92).

Abortion is a concern for teenagers who engage in un-Christian sexual behaviours. They try to terminate the life of the un-born baby from the womb. This is why the WHO defines abortion as a procedure for terminating an unintended pregnancy either by persons lacking the necessary skills or in an environment lacking the minimal medical standard, or both. In its estimation of unsafe abortion, the WHO rated Eastern Africa as having 2.4 million young mothers, 930,000 for Middle East, 900.000 for Northern Africa, 120.000 for Southern Africa and 1.8 million for West Africa where Nigeria resides. In all, Africa is rated 39 % of teenage unintended pregnancies as at 2008 (Mesce and Clifton, 2011: 3-5).

Recently, a doctor gynaecologist disclosed in the Leadership Newspaper dated October 4, 2015, and he said:

You will be amaze to know the number of teenagers that are brought to hospitals for abortion or D and C by parents and guardians. The rate is quite alarming and for teen pregnancy, the problem is always the fact that they are pregnant and they are not prepared for it, or they will bring shame to their families. Teen pregnancy is generally defined as pregnancy occurring in a young woman between the ages of 13 and 17, or in anyone who is not legally considered an adult. And these have consequences parent don't even care about. Some of the negative effects include death, because their bodies are still developing. There are lots of complications and these could be hemorrhage, sepsis and injuries to pelvic and intra-abdominal (Yunusa, 2015:1).

This again, is a growing concern when a young girl of 12-19 of age gets pregnant in that School age. Usually, there will be serious confusion. Such confusion may be due to physical immaturity of the teenager, perceived social effect, and economic factors which accompany pregnancy at an early age.

A preliminary visit to the field of this research reveals a young girl of 15 who confided to say she had aborted once without the knowledge of her parents and that she has not been able to keep to one sex partner since then. According to her, she went for the abortion because of fear not to be rejected by family and friends. For her, she felt it was going to be a thing of shame if the pregnancy was exposed to the point of delivery. This teenager is said never to be aware of the complications from the result of unsafe abortion. This is to say the parent had never had such discussion with her. There are usually unhealthy implications with unsuccessful abortions. Some of the consequences of unsafe abortion could include loss of productivity, economic burden on public health system, stigma & long-term health problems such as infertility.

Early or Forced Marriage

Sometimes when premarital sex results into a pregnancy, the parents of those who are involved may just propel them to get married even when they are too young for marriage. In most cases, this pressure comes from the parents of the girl because they would not want to harbour their unmarried pregnant daughter in their house. More so, youths involved in premarital sexual relationship may feel compelled to remain in the relationship and get married even though there are doubts of compatibility.

School Drop Out

Unwanted pregnancy often disrupts the education of female youths, thereby increasing the chances of dropping out of school. When a girl becomes pregnant and drops out of school, she may never resume again except in rare cases. Even when the girl decides to remain in school, the challenges of unplanned pregnancy and motherhood may lead to poor academic performance. This has prevented many individuals from achieving their educational goals. Consequently, poverty may set in because job opportunities have decreased as a result of lack of education on the part of the teenager.

Purpose of the Study

Besides being an academic requirement for the award of the Degree, Bachelor of Arts in Theology (Christian Education), specifically, this learning is to:

1. Examine the extent of parental involvement in sex education in Kishika community.

2. Ascertain why are parents unwilling to be involved in the sex education of teenagers in Kishika community

3. Determine Why are parents willing to be involved in sex education of teenagers in Kishika

4. Examine the challenges that parents face in their involvement in sex education of teenagers in Kishika

5. Determine what type of support would help parents be better involved in sex education of teenagers in Kishika.

Significance of the Problem

This research look at the level of Kishika parents' involvements in their teenagers' sex education. The research shall outline the need for parents' involvement in teenager's sex education with Biblical principles, and point out some dangers to watch against the lack of involvement. The research shall consider the parents level of involvement in achieving a comprehensive sexuality education. The focus in this section shall be on the parental involvement in addressing the teenager's psychological and spiritual dimensions of sexuality for the cognitive domain (information), good moral values and attitude, communication and decision making skill of the teenager.

Definition of Terms

For the purpose of clearer understanding of the thesis, some key terms that might appear on the research will be clearly defined under the context of this learning. The researcher therefore has defined the following terms to aid the understanding of the study:

Parental Involvement

This can be seen as a deliberate act of a parent to build good and communicative relationship with his or her teen.

Sex Education

This can be seen in the context of this learning as the acquirement of information that helps teenagers to make informed decisions and beliefs about sex, sexual affections, sexual developments, physical body change, sexually transmitted diseases, and consequences of teenage sexual involvements.

Parental Willingness

This is the agreement and acceptance of a parent to pass on sex information to teenagers under his or her care.

Parental Unwillingness

This is an act of disagreement and un-acceptance of a parent to pass on sex information to teenagers under his or her care.

Research Questions

The study has tried to answer the following questions:

1. What is the extent of parental involvement in sex education of teenagers in Kishika?

2. Why are parents finding it difficult to be involved in sex education of teenagers in Kishika?

3. Why are parents interested in being involved in sex education of teenagers in Kishika?

4. What are the challenges parents faces in their involvement in sex education of teenagers inKshika?

5. What type(s) of support would help parents to be better involved in sex education of teenagers in Kishika?

Delimitation of the Study

This study focused on evaluating parental involvement on sex education in Kishika community. Also, parental involvement is looked at from the biblical perspective. The entire study therefore, is delimited in terms of parents' involvement only, parents of teenagers only in the sex education of their teenagers, parent involvement in sex education in terms of teenager's decisions and beliefs about sex, sexually transmitted diseases, and consequences of teenage sexual involvements in Kishika community. The Kishika community is a growing community that has teenagers as the majority. A good number of these teenagers especially girls have dropped out of school because of teenage pregnancy. Again, to the best of the researcher's knowledge, there has not been any held sex education program or existing written available study on sex education in Kishika community.

Summary

It is seen that chapter one is an introductory chapter which serves as a guide to the subsequent chapter. It is also understood that the work is going to be both literal and oral interview research on parent's involvement on their teenager's sex education. This chapter therefore focuses on the general introduction. Statement of problem, purpose of the study, significance of the study, definition of terms, research questions, delimitation of the study and summary of the chapter.

CHAPTER TWO

LITERATURE REVIEW

Introduction

The researcher in this particular section will attempt to review necessary resource materials which will be relevant to this research. In doing so, the researcher will search what the bible has to say, and what other authors have written on parental involvement in sex education.

Overview of Sex Education

The term sex education is used throughout this thesis to refer to home-based educational programs which are carried out by parents. The focus is on teenage sexuality, sexuality and sexual decision-making which should be discussed and supervised by parents, although the term is often considered inadequate to describe the full range of attitudinal and behavioural factors that need to be addressed (Alldred, and Epstein 2003:80-97). The issue of sexuality education has become an extremely divisive matter. The mere mention of it attracts several questions and positions of interest. But before the research state some of the general positions, there is need to clarify and give some definitions from writers.

Sexuality education as defined by McGrath and Congoire is the various sexuality related aspects of human life including the physical and psychological developments, behaviours, attitudes, and social customs associated with the individual sense of gender, relationship, sex, and culture thereby, setting humans apart from other members of the animal kingdom in which the objective of sexuality is more often confined to reproduction (McGrath & Congoire, 1983). On the other hand, sexuality education provides young people with the knowledge, skills and efficacy to make informed decisions about their sexuality and lifestyle (Michel, 2009:1). This then brings to fore the educational responsibility of parents in helping teenagers in acquiring information, understand their sexual body developments and uniqueness as well as learn about sexual transmitted diseases, sexual health and behaviour, consequences of teenage sex, unwanted pregnancy, and abortion among others.

Information from Parents to Teenagers

Every teenager needs information from parent on the matters of sex education so as to develop positive attitudes and values for sex. They need to know that sex in itself is not a devilish activity. According to Dobson "sex is not dirty and it is not evil" (1978:2). However, to be involved in sexual activity before marriage happens to be morally unacceptable for the Christian community. If such information is gotten from parents, it helps the teenager to form appropriate sexual attitudes and beliefs. In a situation whereby there is inadequate parental involvement in the sex education of teenagers, the resultant effect can be negative sex attitudes, values and beliefs by teenagers. Parents are responsible to relate sexual information to teenagers. Tim and Mark shed more light in their work when they said, "there is no substitute for every hour, minute, and second of quality time parents spend with their children. They need heavy doses of their parents, everyday if possible, and they need the modeling and the direct instruction that only a parent can give…(to) maintaining good sexual relations" (2010:244-245). Parental involvements help the teenager to be trained in responsible sexual attitudes.

Teenage Sexuality

The concept of sexual uniqueness is for parents to help teenagers understand their sexual unique nature and affections. God has uniquely made teenagers for His purpose (Ps 139). Parents are to see them as unique human beings created and structured by God. Sally Wehmeier defines teenagers as boys and girls between 13 and 19 years (Wehmier, 2006:1520). The age between 13 and 19 of a teenager have some physical uniqueness and development that takes place and might not be hidden from parents. The Palo Alto Medical Foundation gives a more objective picture as it stressed that teenagers usually transits into three different stages of experiences as they grow: the physical, cognitive and personality changes (2011: 2). The foundation further explained the changes in boys and girls as:

> In girls, body fat increases, breast begins to expand, pubic hair grows, height and weight increases, first menstrual period begins, hip widens, skin and hair becomes more oily and then pimples on the face may begin to appear. For the boys, scrotum becomes darker, and grow larger, penis grow longer and fuller, pubic hair grows, breast can get tender, height and weight increases, muscles develop, wet dreams occurs, voice cracks and get deeper, skin and hair becomes more oily, pimples may appear, and then under arm and facial hair begins to grow (2011:4).

When parents become aware of these realities they become better informed to be involve in the sexuality education of their teenagers. Parents are to help teenagers' access information about themselves. This is because the teens sometimes might not be aware of what is going on with them. According to Dobson, "As your body starts to change, you will notice that you are beginning to be more interested in people of the opposite sex. Suddenly girls begin to look great to boys and boys starts appealing to girls" (Dobson, 1982: 79, 80).

The above might be the reasons parents may just discover that their teenagers suddenly begin to have desire for sex. They begin to have affection and likeness for members of the opposite sex. Teenagers sometimes may be carried away with excitements of the changes, especially when they see hair growing on their faces. They try to learn how to shave, put on bra, and wear pads among others. Palo Alto Medical Foundation further expatiated on the teen's social and emotional growth to reflect as follows:

> Teenagers begin to spend more time with their peers at the expense of their family members, they begin to change their clothing, wear and change new hair styles, becomes moody in search for self identity. Sometimes they may even begin to contemplate whether to break away from their parents or even get into fight with parent with the parent influence of alcohol or drug – may even see them skipping school just to express his grieve (Palo, 2011:5).

Health

In this age where there are diseases of different names, Nigeria is no different from other countries in the types of sexually transmitted diseases. Parents need to help in informing teenagers about sexually transmitted diseases like syphilis, HIV/AIDs, sexual cancers among others. Teenagers by these should be able to abstain from sexual relations that can cost their lives. Kore added to this and he says, "Abstinence still remains the wisest decision. It ensures health, security, joy, happiness and victory for youth who are tempted in area of sexuality. All other options lead to sickness, gloom, defeat, disgrace destruction" (2004:75). It is healthier for a teenager to wait until marriage before sex. The teenager should be made to know that giving in to sexual lust and temptation can lead to sin and death (Jas 1:14-15).

Parents should instruct in order to direct the mind of the teenager on things that are good and holy instead of sexual affections that are inappropriate. Some teenagers might not be aware of their unique stages of affections. It could be that period of development whereby there may be high sexual feelings for the opposite sex. Parents are to help the teenagers at that time know that there are triggers for sex which teenagers must be aware. These developers could be in form of holding hands, embracing and kissing, all these could arouse sexual desires. According to McDowell, speaking on sexual intercourse among youth says "sexual activities arise among young people on gradual processes" (Sean, McDowell 2005:7, 8). Parents then should note and talk to their teenagers at sensitive period when a teenager begins to desire to go out on a date, desire to hold hands of a boy or a girl, desires to go into romantic activities with the opposite sex, show themselves in public gathering. Akintoye in agreement with the concept says "such juvenile social rituals tend to create an atmosphere for interpersonal affection, love which may even result to sexual activities" (Akintoye, 1987:87).

Origin of Sexuality Education

Sexuality education came into being in different countries at various times. As far back as 1897 in Sweden a female Swedish doctor, Karolina Widerstorm, saw the need to educate the young teenagers especially the girls about sexual hygiene as a way of informing and protecting them from sexually transmitted diseases such as gonorrhoea and syphilis which were found to be very common during that period. To her, the idea was that, "if girls got to know in good time how pregnancy came about and how sexually transmitted diseases were spread, they would be better able to protect themselves. In this way girls were considered to be able to take responsibility for the sexual health for boys as well as for themselves" (Lena, 2000:87). Given the divisive nature of sexuality education at that time, the high prevalence of sexually transmitted diseases was used as the basis of introducing sexuality education in the schools. Despite all the optimistic potentials of sexuality education, the major challenges were what form sexuality should take and at what level it should be introduced in the schools. There was also the problem of methodology. From the researcher's personal observation, some of the religious leaders who are also parents in the Nigerian context viewed sexuality education as non spiritual hence should not be talked about. There is the fear that it could lead to sexual intelligence and insensitivity among the teenagers. The adolescent recipients of sexuality education were therefore viewed as bad boys and girls.

In Nigeria, traditional forms of sexuality education existed in kinship systems and coming-of-age ceremonies where the youth were tutored about manhood and womanhood. Its essence was purely biological and culture detailed. There were various methods of contraceptives which included virginity, herbs, breastfeeding, the ring, and abstinence; most of which were strictly meant for the married and kept as a secret. Issues on sexually transmitted diseases were also of great concern but were barely discussed while the contraction of them was a big shame and stigma. The socialization process of the child remained strictly the only way of acquainting the child with issues like family relationships and public manners with very little room for self-expression.

The fast pace of urbanization encouraged rapid improvement in communication and transportation which had tremendous effect on sexuality issues in Nigeria. The use of telephones and letters helped to promote interpersonal relationships. The print media intensified and popularized the notion of flirting, dating and a variety of sexual behaviours. Intimate relationships developed from social activities such as dancing, singing and local drama sketches. In spite of these changes, information on sexuality was still kept secret, not openly discussed, and was perceived as dirty or evil particularly by religious leaders who often viewed morality as being determined by a higher order from above (Adepoju, 2005). Three types of sex education programs are Abstinence Sex education, HIV education program, and Comprehensive Sex education.

Abstinence Sex Education

This is the type of sex education that talks more of holding oneself from any form of sexual intercourse, typically until marriage. The purpose of this teaching according to LarTelfim Damson "it is to bring about morality, social, psychological and health gains realization" (LarTelfim, 2010:4). This is to teach abstinence from sex activity outside marriage as a standard for teenagers, this will then help them to avoid pregnancy outside marriage and sexual transmitted diseases. Abstinence encourages teenagers to reject sexual advances by the opposite sex outside marriage. It promises to benefit the teenager rather than engaging in sex before marriage. Lar says that "those who reserve sexual intercourse for marriage often enjoy more satisfying sex and more stability in their marriages" (2010:4). Again, Kirby identified abstinence-only sex education programs as that program that "focus on abstinence from sexual intercourse, typically until marriage" as the only method of preventing unwanted pregnancy and/or the spread of STDs while abstinence-plus sex education programs that teach abstinence as well as the use of contraceptives to prevent pregnancy and the spread of STDs (1997: 25). Abstinence is a wise decision; it promotes healthy and secured sexual life. Without abstinence, teenagers may be open to sickness, pregnancy outside marriage and disgraceful testimonies. According to Avert, a supporter of abstinence-only sex education view sex outside of marriage as immoral and reject the provision of information about how to use condoms as wrong because it sends a "mixed message." In addition, they claim teens who abstain from sex are less likely to be depressed, commit suicide, or live in poverty (Avert, 2008:20).

Abstaining from sex is taught as a strategy to reduce unintended pregnancy and STD/HIV in teens in all sex education programs; however, when abstinence is the only method taught, it is referred to as "abstinence-only" education. Abstinence-only education does not discuss condoms and birth control unless it is to mention failure rates (Darroch, 2000:204).This aspect of sexuality education does not welcome reproductive health education like that of comprehensive sexuality education; it may not appreciate discussions on safe sex or birth control for teenagers. The basic practice under this type of sex education is that the teenager may refrain from any act of sexual activity until marriage. He or she may not discuss contraceptive nor condom use and its implications. This is confirmed by John Santelli, who says Abstinence from sexual intercourse represents a healthy choice for most teenagers, as they face considerable risk to their reproductive health from unintended pregnancy and sexually transmitted infections (STIs) including infection with the human immunodeficiency virus (HIV).

Remaining abstinent at least through high school is usually supported by parents and even by adolescents themselves (Santelli, 2006: 83). For Santelli, abstinence only sexuality is an important behavioural strategy for avoiding STIs and unwanted pregnancy among teens. Sexually active teenagers face considerable risk to their reproductive health from unintended pregnancy and STIs including infection with HIV. Santelli, continues when he admits that abstinence only sexuality is an educational or motivational program which has its exclusive purpose as, teaching the social, psychological, and health gains which can be realized. According to Santelli, such abstinence is the expected standard for all school-age children. The abstinence only program teaches that abstinence from sexual activity as a teenager is one of the ways to avoid out of wedlock pregnancy, sexually transmitted diseases, and other associated health problems. Santelli also opines that a mutually faithful monogamous relationship in the context of marriage is the expected standard of human sexual activity. Again, he teaches that sexual activity outside of the context of marriage is likely to have harmful psychological and physical effects. Furthermore, he postulated that bearing children out-of-wedlock is likely to have shameful consequences for the child, the child's parents, and the extended family (Santelli, 2006: 84). Abstinence-only sexuality programs sometime may have some disadvantages. By its practice, it looks coercive and does not give full information, it seem to have the tendency of withholding some aspect of information needed for teenagers to make informed choices when it comes sexuality.

Some culturally oriented Nigerian parents who may like to settle for Abstinence- Only Programs, probably because of cultural beliefs. It however noted that as human beings, sexuality is part of one's identity. Again, it is obvious that sexuality education includes many aspects of life not only sexual intercourse. Comprehensive sexuality education teaches intimacy, human relationships, sexual identity and gender roles, reproductive anatomy and body image, puberty and the reproductive, the struggle of stress, peer pressure, drugs, relationships, and sexual decision-making. On the other hand, abstinence only programs promote 'no-sex' as the only way to go. These programs include conversations about character building and values, but they neglect reality. Teenagers do have sex, even Kids are continuing to try sex at an ever more tender age: more than 1/3 of 15-year –old boys have had sexual intercourse, as have 27% of 15-year-old girl (Gibbs, 1993: 61) and telling them to just say no is not going to change their minds. Not only are these teens having sex, but they are obviously having defenceless intercourse that is prone to disease attack.

HIV/AIDS Sexual Education Program

HIV/AIDS is an epidemic in parts of the world today. It is one of the effects of unprotected sexual activities. The HIV education is a program that is strategically planned by health workers with the help of parents in communities to help teenagers get oriented on the dangers of multiple sex partners and perceived risk of HIV. HIV education through parents can go as far as helping teenagers in changing sexual attitudes and behaviours. Parents must educate teenagers to return to God's standards of sexual purity and abstinence before marriage. God still expects that both husband and wife remain faithful to one another sexually. By so doing, sexual diseases like HIV can be prevented to a great extent.

Comprehensive Sex Education

The United Nations who are supporters of comprehensive sex education believe it is a basic human right to have access to information about matters affecting teens and the decisions they make. These supporters assert sex education provides young people with the means to protect themselves against abuse and exploitation, unintended pregnancies, STDs, and HIV (Office of the United Nations, 1998). The United Nations goal is to be sensitive to all religions, but did not base its sex education on any set of specific religious values. Comprehensive Sexuality Education emphasizes a holistic approach to human development and sexuality. UNESCO identifies the primary goal of sexuality education as "children and young people become equipped with the knowledge, skills and values to make responsible choices about their sexual and social relationships in a world affected HIV" (UNESCO. 2009). The International Planned Parenthood Federation (IPPF) defines a rights based approach to comprehensive sexuality education as:

> To equip young people with the knowledge, skills, attitudes and values they need to determine and enjoy their sexuality – physically and emotionally, individually and in relationships. Comprehensive sexuality education is an approach that recognizes and promotes human rights, knowledge, values and skills necessary for HIV prevention, and gender equality (IPPF, 2011:3).

One of the types of sex education adopted in Nigeria so far is the International Planned Parenthood Federation (IPPF). This is an education process that is designed to assist young people in their physical, social, emotional and moral development as they prepare for adulthood, marriage, parenthood and ageing. It also includes teenagers' social relationship in the socio-cultural context of family and society (IPPF, 1987:3).

By implication, one goal of comprehensive sexuality education is to tell the teenagers the truth about sexuality so as to moderate sexual problems in the society. Some teenagers could be knowledgeable about sexuality but ignorant of the implications. If parents are not involved in teaching or telling teenagers the real implication, they may end up getting incorrect and distorted sexual information without knowing the implications. Parents at this point, get involved in finding out what the teenagers already know about sexuality, and then add to their knowledge. For instance, if ever they heard and believed that there is cure for AIDS, it is important for parents to correct such mistaken belief through comprehensive sexuality education. This is important because some individuals today encourage young teenagers to engage in premarital sex. For instance, Wardell in his book encourage teenagers to "be warm, open, responsive, and sexually unafraid" (Wardell, 1991:26). For him, sexual intercourse for boys should be seen as only a learning experience, and not something to be afraid. He encourages girls to be sexually experimental because it serves as training and also improves their sex lives eventually when they are married.

Parental involvement in the teenagers' sexuality hence helps to kick against as well as correct such views on sexuality. Teenagers need to get physical, emotional reality information about them. Sometimes when they go through puberty, they may be ignorant of the changes associated. They may not know details of conception, birth control, sexual signals and available contraceptives. It is therefore the responsibility of the parents to sit the teenager down and educate by giving these sexual diversities. Through comprehensive sexuality education, the teenagers are helped to protect themselves from unhelpful results like abortion, infections, sudden pregnancies and sexually transmitted diseases among others. It also helps teenagers to protect themselves from been deceived sexually. Adequate and correct information of sexuality are given by parents so that teenagers can lead a responsible sexual life. In this case, they may know that just one single unprotected sexual act has the tendency of changing their lives negatively- in terms of pregnancies, sexually transmitted disease or sometimes death.

Sources of Sexuality Educations

Sexuality educations usually begin at home. Teachable moments and opportunities to discuss sexuality issues with teens occur on a daily basis. From the moment of birth, children ordinarily begin to learn about love through touch and relationships. Infants learn about sexuality when their parents talk to them, dress them, show affection, play with them, and teach them the names of the parts of their bodies. And as children grow into teenage age, they begin to have knowledge on sexuality through their social relationships with the environment. Parents are to complement such knowledge in sincere and open communication with their teens. This could help lay a good foundation into matured sexually healthy adults.

Apart from the home, teenagers learn about sexuality from other sources like friends, teachers, neighbours, television, music, books, magazine, billboard advertisement and the internet. Parents might not know when all these take place hence; they have to engage their teenagers in friendly communication in order to know what is going on with them.

Biblical Basis for Sex Education

The researcher here will attempt to lay biblical foundation on sex education and how obedience to the bible can inform parents on their involvement towards sex education with their teenagers. The researcher will in addition use the bible to explain what God has in mind concerning children education in the home. Parents are endowed with the responsibility of raising children especially teenagers in this context according to His design. It is believed in the researcher's culture (Igala) that every child born into the world is God's; parents are just tools for caring and nurturing. But then, it is not possible for one to nurture a child without getting involved with the child in terms of education through communication. According to Robert Clark:

> Education for the early Hebrews focused on learning about God. The Bible's opening statement leaves no room for flexibility regarding its main topic (Gen.1:1). God controlled the events in the lives of His people; He initiated the covenants and law; He rose up leaders to instruct His people regarding personal and corporate righteousness. And when a generation failed to follow God's truth, turmoil inevitably followed (Exod 1; Judg 2:10-15) (Robert, 1991:15).

The leaders God has decided to raise within the home circle are the parents. Their basic responsibility is instruction, especially to the children and teenagers that God has given them. As seen in the book of Genesis, sex is God's idea. Genesis 1:27-28 reads, "So God created man in His own image, in the image of God he created him male and female he created them" (NIV). The bible again says, "They were both naked, the man and his wife, and were not ashamed" (Gen 2:25 NKJV). As natural and emotional beings, they were capable of expressions. This is the basis for which Danfulani Kore asserts that "sexuality comes from God and it is part of God's creation to mankind" (Kore, 2004:71). The Old Testament in Genesis 4:1 hereby reaffirms sex when it says "Adam lay with his wife Eve and she became pregnant…" (NIV.1996). The King James Version says "Adam knew his wife and she bore Cain and Abel" (KJV). Kunhiyop alluded to this, in his effort to interpret the passage and he says "the word knew does not mean merely an intellectual awareness of the woman by the man, it means that he had intimate knowledge of her" (Kunhiyop, 2004:292). The New Testament is not left out when Jesus said "the two will become one flesh" (Matt 19:5). Hebrew 13:4 instructed that the marital bed must not be defiled. Paul also recognized sex when he advised that married couples could withhold sex from each other only for a time and for the purpose of prayer (1 Cor 7:5).

From the foregoing biblical concept of sex, it can be clearly seen that even though God created sex, he did that within the marriage union. Sex is biblically accepted when is carried out between husband and wife. This is to say, God condemns sexual immorality. That can be seen in several passages of the Scriptures like Genesis 20:3, Exodus 20:14, Proverbs 6:32-33, Jeremiah 5:7 and 8 among others. As good as sex is from the biblical point, it should be known that there are tendencies that it can be misused especially among teenagers. The bible gives clear example of how people fell into sexual sins. We see the case of Samson and David in the Bible. It is obvious that parents of various cultures have their different beliefs and orientations about sex but that should not stop them from discussing sex with teenagers early enough to help their future experience. If the bible has made the issue of sex clear, parents should also make it clear to their teens. As we see today, there are implications of teenage and unprepared sexuality. These are sexually transmitted disease, abortion, teenage pregnancy, dropping out of school, single parenting and above all, disobedience to God as seen Galatians 5:19-20 and Ephesians 5:3-12.

With these clear implications of inappropriate teenage sexual involvements, parents are therefore given the responsibility by God to father and mother teenagers in such a way that glorifies him. The concern is the parents absent syndrome which teenagers may likely be experiencing in some homes. Parents might not necessarily stay all day with their teens, and they don't also have to be non involving parents with their teenagers. It therefore behoves parents to get close to their teenagers and educate where necessary. According to Johann Arnold:

Parents who neglect to take an active interest in their children because they are 'too busy' do them an injustice. Children long for contact with their parents. Most will not be able to verbalize this longing, perhaps, and some may not even be conscious of it, but it is there in every child. As parents, we must always be ready to answer it (Arnold, 2009:105).

Apart from providing food, good shelter, clothing and medical care for teenagers, parents are to educate their teens against harmful behaviours and decision that could be detrimental to their future endeavours. Apart from parental efforts of parents to educate their children or teenagers, they really need to depend on God for His grace for leading the children. According to Harold Sala, "God is still in the business of helping parents who are committed to Him, asking His help and following the guidelines of scripture" (Sala, 2001: vi). Sexuality parenting is also a calling that should be put into consideration by all parents who wish their teenagers a healthy sexuality future.

Christians tenets of human sexuality traditionally take its orientation from the Bible where it is believed that human genders are ordered by the Creator to be male and female and that human sexual expression is oriented to be male-female copulation. The writer of Genesis (1:27), says, "male and female he created them". This is the root of Christian understanding of human genders and sexuality. The Bible provides details of sexuality in various forms. From the pages of the Bible there are narrations bordering on such themes as exploration of the beauty of the human body, and its sensuous nature. Also, in its genres are to be found stories of incest, polygamy and women who married rapists. It is also taken as given in the Bible that immutable sexual roles were assigned divinely and so are the approved orientations for the sexes. The exact meaning and nuances of these terms were not clearly elaborated in it, but the general picture is that the Bible gives approval only for male-female relationships.

While is it true that the Bible states that sexuality and sex were created by God, yet texts on variations found in human beings have not been clearly noted. The biblical discourse of human nature, sexual identity and gender are tailored towards males and females and does not tell us about another possibility of exhibiting human sexuality. Though nature and archaeological data revealed that hermaphrodites, bisexuals, lesbians, cross-dressers, etc. existed at the biblical periods, which the biblical authors ought to be aware of, but they were ignored. Amidst these scenarios, yet no approval was given to same-sex relationships in the Bible.

New trends in sexual orientations among African Christians

The study notes that despite the general ban of other forms of sexual activities outside malefemale relationships both in traditional African culture and the Bible, the study identifies the presence of "new" sexual orientations among African Christians. The study identifies three prominent forms of "new" sexual trends among African Christians, namely cross-dressing, gay/lesbianism and *transgenderism*. Cross-dressing is used here to refer to the practice of males and females who choose to dress like the opposite sex as a normal way of dressing. This is different from dressings at theaters and for religious purposes. Gay/lesbianism, is here defined as the sexual orientation and practice of sexual expressions of human beings towards their own gender instead of the opposite gender. *Trangenderism* is construed here as the permanent change of one's gender through medical surgery to become the opposite gender.

Taking Nigeria as a case study, the paper notes that few youths of Christian background have become popular cross-dressers. They make public their new orientation on social media. Names of eleven most popular cross dressers in Nigeria obtained from https://ke.opera.news are Booga Barbie, Pleasure Suarez, Remy Lekun, James Brown, Onyx Godwin, Jay Buggati, Iche, JP Blush, Josh Agai, Jay Boogie, Denrele and Bobrisky. Their names, apart from the last, point to a Christian identity, though it is superfluous to be categorical on religious affiliations among African youth in the current clime. An important anthropological point to be noted is that, they are domiciled in the southern part of Nigeria where Christianity dominates. In the northern part of Nigeria, where Islam is more pronounced no cross-dresser or transgender or homosexual has openly made such confession, though studies indicate the presence of homosexuals in that part of the country (Lashima, 2021). In general, cross-dressers are coming out in the Christian dominated areas of Africa.

Lesbians and gays present a different picture from the above. While some Africans are coming out and freely expressing their lesbian sexual orientation, the fact is that they have not been well tolerated in almost all parts of Africa, with the clear exception of South Africa. They are confronted with disdain, abuse and even threatened with death. In Nigeria, the social media also identifies popular transgender of Nigerian origin as Stephanie Rose, Miss Sahara, Noni Salma, Rizi Xavier Timane, Mandy la Candy, Bryan Nwakoro. They are however domiciled in Europe, due to the fear of molestation in Nigeria. Buchi, however lives in Nigeria.

Convergence of African culture and biblical perspectives on human sexuality and gender

The study reveals the striking similarities between traditional African cultures and the Bible on human sexuality, gender roles and sexual expressions. It can be stated as of first importance that both cultures have hallowed traditions of sexuality. Africans have traditional tenets on sexuality and gender, that are hallowed and scholars like Asare, (2014), Obiero, (2010) and Ukpokolo (2010) have elucidated the themes. These are coded in their culture, sayings, proverbs, songs and drama and dances. The Bible in its narratives also presents what can be called approved basic norms of sexuality and gender.

The paper identifies and explores the convergence of traditional African perspectives and biblical understanding of human sexuality and gender, and points out that they are closely related and are oriented towards the same purposes. The study surmises them under these themes: (i) male-female intersex, (ii) meant for procreation, (iii) enjoyment, (iv) companionship, (v) music and pun. The study opines that the two have similar perspectives on human sexuality, though each has traits that are peculiar:

(i) Male-female intersex: Africans in general hold that humanity is sharply divided into male and female. The Yoruba say, *"tiako, ti abo niadaile aye"* (male and female is the order of creation of the world). This is the same opinion from the Bible and orthodox Christianity, as the Bible states, "male and female he created them" (Genesis 1:27). However, human reality shows that there are admissions of abridgment of the sexes that are normal in biology but traditionally called aberrations which contradicts the two sharp divisions. The *genderisation* of humanity into male and female is so sacrosanct in traditional African culture and in the Bible, that known abridgment or hybridization of these forms of human sexuality is usually hidden and despised.

(ii) Procreation: Traditional African societies believe that human sexuality is importantly meant for procreation. In a culture where celibacy is discountenanced, the inability to engage in procreative activities is considered a great crime against the lineage and community. Individuals in traditional African communities as norms are expected to contribute to the continuum of his/her lineage by using his/her sexuality to increase the population. This same idea is found in the Bible, where the Creator states "increase and multiply, fill the earth..." (Genesis 2: 28). Exegetically, it is generally agreed that human sexuality was ordered for human procreation, which imposes a duty on human beings as willing co-creators, (Woggen, 1981; Huber and Graybill, 2020).This duty is so sacrosanct in the Bible that dereliction of it was considered a major crime. The case of Onan who engaged in *coitus interruptus* was considered a mortal sin against the community of Israel, (Genesis 38) and was punished with instant death.

(iii) Conjugal rights: Another aspect of human sexuality found both in the Bible and traditional African societies is that sex is a conjugal right to be engaged by a man and woman and it is meant for human enjoyment. This is stated in *oduOdi-Mejiof Ifa.* Due to this factor, moral rules were imposed on the society to guide and moderate its usage among the population. Thus, both the Bible and traditional African norms assert that sexual activity must necessary take place between men and women, to the total exclusion of mating with animals or effigies. Heterosexual relationship is the approved form of mating in African culture, (as specifically stated in Ifaoracle) and also by the Church. The Catholic, Code of Canon Law, (CCC, 1055), defines marriage as "a covenant of man and woman", who are obliged to conjugal rights.

(iv). Companionship: Human intersexuality was considered to be made in such a way as to enhance companionship and friendship. Intersex friendship is considered necessary for the growth of the human society. According to Ifa, in *oduOsa-Ika*, and *oduOdi-Meji*, Olodumare (God) frowns at same sex relationships. Ifa states that, at a stage which was very early in human history, women conspired to withdraw into "women community", however, that at the intervention of Orunmila, a Yoruba principal deity, women started paring themselves up with men. By the following year, they have started giving birth to children and then began to multiply in number". The Bible equally enjoins companionship as a factor of male-female relationship. According to Genesis (2: 18), "It is not good for man to be alone", hence the Creator formed a woman as a companion of man.

(v) Music and pun: Human sexuality has been used and it is being used as a means of entertainment. People compose songs and lyrics in traditional African societies about genders, beauty, sexual parts, lusciousness, and even abusive songs on sexual offenders, and sexual deviants. The Bible contains sensuous lyrics such as the book Song of Songs, which has explicit scenes of intimacy, lyrics of beauty and sexual expressions.

Summary and Recommendations

The paper examines the dilemma of Africa Christians in the face of modern influence on sexuality. It studies the convergence in traditional African societies and the Bible on human sexuality. The study opines that the two cultures share striking simulacrum on human sexual tenets. Thus, due to these similarities and the demands by both cultures as discussed above, an African Christian would be at home with his/her sexuality either as an African or and as a Christian. The study also reveals that Christianity in Africa and indeed all religions on the continent are exposed to new trends in intersexuality and in the roles of the sexes. The study underscores the fact that some African Christians are expressing radical sexual orientations, which befuddled their communities. The presence of westernization and its education, globalization and its media have brought new trends to sexual orientation in public among African Christians, which are termed unconventional orientations. These trends are alien to the moral rights of African parents' guidance on wards as they grow up.

The paper observes that another way in which modern African Christians are expressing their sexuality in new forms is in their dressing and general lifestyle. Also, new words have entered African lexicon, like same-sex marriage, cohabitation, trial marriages, and even gay bishops/priests, etc., which are now common in conversations and acts than hitherto experienced. The study notices on-going obscurantic notions of sexuality such that words like maleness and femaleness as applied to dressing and occupations are converging and no longer clear-cut. The study underscores that clear cut terms like males and females are being challenged by Christian transgenders and cross dressers. The activities of cross-dressers and transgenders and lesbians are generally under doses of foreign influence. Modern African Christians and church ministers at liturgical, private and public functions adorn revealing clothes. It can be stated that in comparison with their Muslim counterparts in Africa, modern African Christians are more daring in dressing.
The study surmises that under the claims of globalization and modernism, the activities of gays and lesbian and transgender are characterized by more

openness than hitherto. The issue of public approval versus disapproval remains contentious in Africa for homosexuals and transgender. The paper concludes that traditional African culture and the Bible have similar cods on human sexuality. The inroads of modernization, westernization and globalization have brought sharp cultural shocks to African Christians who are forced to contend with their sexuality and its expressions.

In view of the Biblical and African concept of sexuality among Africans, and the subsequent modifications by the colonial agents, the following recommendations are made for proper curbing of the contemporary challenges of sexuality among African people:

I. Sex and sexuality matters should be handled by matured and responsible African parents in order for them to properly teach their wards the does and don't about sexual relationship. Obaje (2020: 1) thinks that male and female, especially young people in Africa need sexuality attention and guidance of parents to help them transit to adulthood. This is because there are so many unAfrican and inaccurate messages about sexuality almost on a daily basis. Parents who are traditional custodians of African morality must gear up with the task of guiding oncoming African generations.

II. The Church and educational institutions should incorporate sexual issues in their teachings at certain stages to help the African youth learn proper things about male and female sexuality and its implications to the individual and the society.

III. Religious bodies and the custodians of African traditions should wisely soft-pedal the taboo placed on the knowledge about human sexuality to help young Africans come out of their hiding place on the issue of sex and sexual relationship and appreciate such in line with the traditional value system.

Against some Eurocentric imagination that the majority of opposite sex relations in Africa would have resulted to indiscriminate sexual activity especially premarital sexual union, there are indications of strict unwritten rules, which usually guide and enforce discipline among African Christians. For instance, in some East African societies where a foreigner may define as having a strong passion for sex, there are indications that failure to adhere to the rules that guide sexual union was an offence against even the society as a whole. According to Okafor (2018), "the openness with which sexuality is expressed does not necessarily mean that sexual activity is indiscriminate among the African societies especially, in the Eastern part. The problem arises where sexuality is evaluated using foreign moral formulation".

Male and female sexuality and sexual relationship have shown up as a physiological cum cultural phenomena. It is physical because it is a naturally occurring urge for pleasure. Again, it is cultural because Africa happens to be a human society which has created for itself a moral value system that determines how individual members of the society participate in any form of relationship or activity especially as regards to sexual relationship. Hence,sex and sexuality in the subconscious mind of Africans has the concept of taboo and sacredness in connection with sexuality. Allowing the imposition of more foreign devastating moral value on African society in the name of cultural globalization, will reduce the African societies to a mere conglomeration of lower infra sentient beings without culture.

Summary

In view of the fact that today the teenager spends almost half of his or her youthful

life in the home, and parents sometimes seem to be absent in terms of

communicative attention to the teenagers' sexuality. Parents should therefore not

create gap between them and their teens. They should get involved in the counsel and education of their teenagers. The paper thus views school-based sexuality education as complementing and augmenting parents, religious and community groups, and health care professionals. This paper contends that the primary goal of sexuality education is to help parents build foundation as they mature into sexually healthy adults. Sexuality education would thus seek to assist teenagers in developing a positive view of sexuality, provide them with information and skills about taking care of their sexual health, helping them to make sound decisions now and in the future. In this way, parents can help in ensuring that future generations have a healthy, respectful, responsible and pleasurable approach to sexuality. Such an enormous task for the parents would mean that they give adequate information.

CHAPTER THREE

RESEARCH METHODOLOGY

Research Design

The research design adopted for this study is a combination of library research and field oral interview. The Byang Kato Library at Jos ECWA Theological Seminary (JETS), University of Jos library, Baptist Theological seminary Kawo Kaduna and internet sources were use for this study. Also, open ended oral interview questions were use for the research. The information collated followed the standard of Jos ECWA Theological Seminary, (JETS) and university of Jos.

41

Participants

The targeted participants are parent of t 41 ·s living in Kishika community, Bassa local Government area Council of Plateau State. A target respondent participants of 30 mothers, and 20 fathers making a total of 50 parents. Out of the 50, 36 parents are members of the Baptist Church Kishika while others belong to other denomination within the communality.

Instrument

There were open ended questions and participants responded based on what they think is the actual situation. After the introduction, part A of the interview asked personal information. There were four items. Part B asked question based on the research questions. There are 5 questions in part B, though one question had parts a, b, and c.

Procedure for Data Collection

The interview will be conducted in Kishika village community, Bassa Local Council Area of Plateau State, Nigeria. The interview lasted for a total period of three days. The oral interview shall be conducted from house to house for 14 parents while 36 parents shall be interviewed in the Baptist Church resident in Kishika. In the case of husband and wife, they shall be interviewed separately for the purpose of openness and confidentiality. However, permission shall be requested from husbands in the case of wife's interview. The interview is recorded using audio recorder. In all, questions will be asked one on one to total number of 50 parents who are members of Kishika community. The participants were briefed about the interview after getting their consent, thereafter the interview began. Where the participant was unable to understand Hausa language, the researcher sought for an interpreter who interpreted to him or her. The two places of meeting the parents were homes and the Kishika Baptist Church auditorium. The interview questions were administered to those who were interested. A total of 50 parents (mothers and fathers) were interviewed and data collected.

Data Analysis

The data analysis is presented using table format. The table is used to analyze

collected data; the collected data are analyzed by the use of simple percentages so as

to determine the percentages of facts in the study.

CHAPTER FOUR

DATA PRESENTATION AND ANALYSIS

Introduction

This chapter presents and analyzes the data as collected from the respondents. The

respondents are a combination of mothers and fathers of teenagers residing in Kishika.

The table 1-4 below shows demographic data of respondents.

Data Presentation, Analysis and Interpretation

Question One

Respondents' length of time as parent

Table 1

44

	Respondents	Frequency	Percentage
Length of time as a parent	5-15 years	20	40%
	16-25	16	32%
	26-30	10	20%
	35 years	4	8%
	Total	50	100

The above table shows that 40% of respondents being the majority have been parents between 5-15 years.

Question Two

Respondents' Educational qualification

Table 2

	Respondents	Frequency	Percentage
Educational qualification	None	17	34%
	Primary	23	46%
	Secondary	8	16%
	Tertiary	2	4%

	Total	50	100

Table 2 shows that46% respondents being the highest are primary school leavers while 34% have never been to school for learning activities.

Question Three

Respondents' Occupation

Table 3

	Respondents	Frequency	Percentage
	Farmer	30	60%
Occupation	Civil Servant	11	22%
	Security Guard	4	8%
	Driver	5	10%
	Total	50	100

The table above shows that 60% of respondents being the majority are farmers. As observed, the result shows that farming is the major occupation of the respondents.

Question Four

Numbers of teen's respondents have

Table 4

	Respondents	Frequency	Percentage
	2-6	27	54%
The number of	7-9	14	28%
teens parent have	10 and above	9	18%
	Total	50	100

Table four above showed that most of the respondents 54% have between 2 - 6 teenagers.

Question Five

The first research question asked, what is the extent of parental involvement in sex education of teenagers in Kishika? The data to answer this research question is presented in the tables below: **whether parents have discussed sexuality issues with their teens.**

Table 5

Responses	Number of Respondents	Percentage
No	38	76%
Not sure	3	6%
Yes	9	18%
Total	50	100%

The table above shows that 76% of respondents have never been involved with their teenagers' sex education. While 6% are not sure, 18% have made effort to address issues of sexuality with their teens

Question Six

The type of sexuality topic parents have discussed with their teenagers.

Table 6

Responses	Number of Respondents	Percentage
None	41	82%
Rules related to dating and contact with opposite sex.	2	4%
HIV AIDS and other sexual related diseases.	3	6%
Unwanted pregnancy and dangers associated with abortion.	4	8%
Total	50	100%

From the percentages of those who discussed types of sexual topics with their teens, 6% discussed HIV AIDS & and other sexual related diseases. However, more parents (8%) had discussed "unwanted pregnancy and dangers associated with abortion" with their teens.

Question Seven

The frequency of sexuality discussion of parents with teenagers.

Table 7

Responses	Number of Respondents	Percentage
Don't talk about it at all	41	82%
Whenever opportunity comes up.	7	14 %
Not sure	2	4%
Total	50	100%

From the result above, 82% of respondents announced their stand not to talk about sexuality even for once to their teens. 14% of parents did discussed sexuality with their teens whenever opportunity arises. 4% of the respondents said they are not sure if they ever discussed sexuality with their teens.

Question Eight

Why it is difficult for parents to discuss sex education with their teens.

Table 8

Responses	Number of Respondents	Percentage
It is against our culture	30	60%
Lack of time	15	30%
Lack of parental knowledge of sex education	5	10%
Total	50	100%

Results from the above table indicate that 60% of respondents are unwilling to be involved in sex education with their teenagers because they feel it is against their culture. 30% are not willing because they don't have the time, they spend their time on the farm and other works to make ends meet. Only 10% of the respondents said they are not willing because they lack the knowledge of sex education.

The data analysis above indicates that 60% out of 100% have taken a stand to maintain cultural tenets against sexuality discussions with teen hence, are unwilling to be involved in sex education with their teens.

Question Nine

Why parents are willing to be involved in sex education with their teens.

Table 9

Responses	Number of Respondents	Percentage
Not willing	39	78%
So as to prevent Unwanted pregnancy and dangers associated with abortion.	5	10%
To prevent teens from HIV AIDS & and other sexual related diseases.	4	8%
To be acquainted with rules related to dating and contact with opposite sex.	2	4%
Total	50	100%

From the table above, 39 parents said they are not willing in being involved in sex education with their teens. Hence, they have no reason why they are not involved in sex education with their teens. 10% said they are willing because they want to prevent their teens from unwanted pregnancy and dangers associated with abortion.

8% are willing because they want to prevent their teens from HIV AIDS & and other sexual related diseases. 4% said they want their teens to be acquainted with rules related to dating and contacts with opposite sex.

Question Ten

Challenges parents faced in their efforts to give sex education to teens.

Table 10

Responses	Number of Respondents	Percentage
No effort to give sex education	36	72%
My teenagers do not feel comfortable discussing sexual issues with me.	9	18%
Teens prefer discussing sexual issues with their friends instead of parent.	5	10%
Total	50	100%

The result above shows that 72% of the respondents had not made any effort to give sex education to their teens. Hence, they have no challenge regarding sex education to their teens. 18% had the challenge of teens not being comfortable to discuss sex related issues with them while 10% are faced with the challenge of teens preferring to talk to friends on sexual issues instead of them.

Question Eleven

The type of support parents want that can help them carry out sex education with their teens.

Table 11

Responses	Number of Respondents	Percentage
Reassurance that sex education is good for teenagers	35	70%
Church base support	9	18%
Not sure	6	12%
Total	50	100%

From the above table, 35% of the respondents admitted to the fact that they want the type of support that reassures them that sex education is good for teenagers even though their culture prohibits it.

CHAPTER FIVE

DISCUSSION, RECOMMENDATIONS AND CONCLUSION

Discussion

The first part of this chapter will discuss the results of the findings found from the demographic information of parents and the research questions of the study. The second part of the chapter will give recommendations for action in the future. Finally, part three will present overall conclusion to the study.

Demographic Information of Parents

The respondents for the interview comprised 50 parents of teenagers. The length of time as parents for most of the respondents is between 5-15 years. The current level of education of most of the respondents is primary school 46% and 34% were not privileged to have gone to school. However, majority of the respondents were farmers 60%. This shows that populations of parents who do farming as occupation are quite high in Kishika.

Extent of Parents' Involvement in Sex Education

The study revealed that 76% of respondents were not involved with their teen's sex education.While the lowest number of respondents6% identified that they were not sure whether they discussed sexuality issues with their teens. The percentage score for the extent of parents' involvement in sex education is 18%; showing low percentage to sex education in Kishika. One can therefore deduce that the respondents probably have never been involved in sex education with their teens because of their cultural misconception about sex education. This is because many of the parents did not discuss sexuality issues with their teens. It therefore indicates that Kishika parents need to understand aspects of sexuality education. Some parents acknowledged they were involved in sexuality education with their teens. Parents need educational orientation against negative attitudes to sex education. That will help them to modify their attitude and perception towards sexuality education. It is expected that Churches and religious leaders be involved in the development of what extent sexuality education takes in and around Kishika. They should be able to embark on spiritual and social actions in a culturally appropriate ways that would motivate parents to regularly begin to discuss sexual issues with their teens in Kishika.

Types of Sexuality Topics Parents

Have Discussed with their Teenagers

Most of respondents 82% did not discuss any sex related topic with their teens. However, 8% discussed unwanted pregnancy and dangers associated with abortion, 6% discussed HIV AIDS and 4% discussed rules related to dating and contact with opposite sex. Majority did not discuss any sexuality topics during their interaction with their teenagers. This can be as a result of their cultural beliefs and perception about sexuality education.

The above findings are supported by a similar report given by UNESCO; it concluded that "one of the common concerns about provision of sexuality education is that sexuality education is against local culture and religion" (UNESCO, 2010). UNESCO further suggests the need for cultural relevance and local adaptation, through engaging and building support among the custodians of culture in a given community. Church and religious leaders in this context must be involved in the development of what form sexuality education takes.

The Frequency of Sexuality

Discussion of Parents with Teenagers

The frequency of sexuality discussion of parents with teenagers was represented by the majority 82% who preferred not to talk about sexuality with their teens at all. Few respondents preferred to discuss it whenever opportunity came 14%. Most respondents do not discuss sexuality with their teens. This could be as a result of their cultural perception of sexuality education; their perception was understood not to be positive. Again, it could be linked to the fact that in the African setting, it is certainly not easy to talk on sexuality. A typical African parent might never be seen talking about sex related issues with their children. As far as some of them are concerned, sex discussion is a realm considered completely a taboo. This is related to Kore's assertion that in Nigeria, "communication between parents and children is generally poor because in many cultures, children do not sit together with their parents, especially their fathers…..children are left on their own until the time they get married" (Kore, 2012:79). As long as there is communication gap between teenagers and parents, it becomes very difficult for sexuality discussions to take place.

Why it is Difficult for Parents to

Discuss Sex Education with their Teens

The result of the findings in research question section B tables 5 showed that majority of the responded admitted that culture is the main cause of the difficulty to discussing sex education with their teens 60%.Meanwhile, those who said their difficulty was lack of parental knowledge of sex educationThe result of the study clearly shows that the major difficulty is a result of the predominance of traditional cultural beliefs; many of the parents still consider that sexual matters are against their cultural standards. The reason for the finding is expressed in Akintunde and Ayantayo research "Sex is considered sacred in all its forms and interpretation. And as a matter of fact, it is something that must not be talked about. Anything that relates to romance and sex should be done secretly" (2005: 4). It is believed here that sexuality is actually a secret affair hence, should not be discussed where teenagers are present.

Why Parents are willing to be

Involved in Sex Education with their Teens

The result shows that 78% of parents are not willing to be involved in sex education with their teens.Relatively few parents gave reasons why they are willing to be involved in sex education with their teens 22%. The first reason was to prevent unwanted pregnancy and dangers associated with abortion 10%, the second is to prevent teens from HIV AIDS and other sexual related diseases 8%, and then to be acquainted with rules related to dating and contact with opposite sex 4%. Religious organization should encourage parents to teach the benefits of teaching sexuality education.The few respondents were aware of the cultural traditions against sexuality education in Kishika but are also faced with the challenges of sexual related issues among their own teens hence they prefer to willingly get involved in their teenage sexuality.

The willingness of the few respondents is in conformity with Oyenike A. Oyinloye's research when she said "sexuality education acquaints the youth with factual and accurate sexual information about the dimension of sexual knowledge that will enable them understand and clarify their personal values and improve their knowledge which will in turn assist them in sexual decision making" (Oyinloye, 2014:2).In support of Oyinloye's conclusion, it is imperative for our religious bodies in this location to be involved in giving orientation using its influence.

Challenges Parents Faced in their

Efforts to give Sex Education to Teens

Some 22% of parents admitted their challenges in the bid to give sex education; the first group said "teenagers do not feel comfortable discussing sexual issues with them"18%,and then the second "teens prefer discussing sexual issues with their friends instead of parents" 10%. Most of the parents had the challenge of not making any effort to give sex education. It is true that some teenagers today might not want to discuss sexuality with their parents, reason being that they worry that parent will misconstrue that they were already sexually active. By that, they prefer to talk sexuality with friends instead of parents. Besides, some of the teenagers might not want parents to label them as immoral therefore; they get uncomfortable discussing sexuality with parents. With the way teenagers begin to think and behave at such times, parents begin to have challenges in talking sexuality with teenagers. These challenges are confirmed in the Alto Medical Foundation research done on young people, which says:

> Teenagers begin to spend more time with their peers at the expense of their family members, they begin to change their clothing, wear and change new hair styles, becomes moody in search for self identity. Sometimes they may even begin to contemplate whether to break away from their parents or even get into fight with parent with the parent influence of alcohol or drug – may even see them skipping school just to express his grieve (Palo, 2011:5).

It can be envisaged that the challenges parents face in their effort to give sex education to teenagers in Kishika would be minimized when parents understand and learn how to communicate with teens in the various stages and periods.

The Type of Support Parents wants that can

Help them carry out Sex Education with their Teens.

Seventy percent of parents want to be reassuredthat sex education is good for teenagers; this is to say the respondents want to be convinced that sex education is good for their teenagers. The finding that parents are ready to be given support about sexuality education with their teens is a useful one in this research. It is imperative that educational effort be made by the Churches with parents so as to have a firm understanding of their sexuality education roles and responsibilities on their teenagers.Though, they have lived and grown in a culture that does not encourage discussions about sexuality. But then, are willing to get to that point of understanding that sex education is good. In the findings, most of the parents are willing to turn to professional support in talking about sex education with their teens. In the context of this study, there are already situations of teenage pregnancy and other sexually related challenges among teenagers. The respondents therefore need the support of organizations especially religious in and outside the community to come and give teachings and orientation as regard the goodness of sexuality education.

Recommendations

Parents should re-evaluate their beliefs that view sexual issues as against their culture by opening up and seeking for religious based help and counsel. In such they can be helped to plan their parenthood in the line of communicating sexuality with their teens. By so doing, they will learn to create the atmosphere for involvement in sex education between them and their teenagers because teens need their involvement.

Based on the fact that some parents do not provide sexual education to the teens because of the fact that it is against their culture and on the other hand ignorance in sexual education matters, there should be Church based sex education program handle by the Churches. The Church should organize parental training that can help the community especially parents learn parenthood in Kishika and then parents will be more involved in sexual education of teens by inculcating in them the moral values so that they can develop safe sex behaviour.

Parents should also be opened to discussions on sexual issues by addressing it in their family, community, and town hall meetings. In such a meeting, members should be allowed to speak out what they feel about sexuality education.

This study discovered difficult living conditions of parents in Kishika. Those parents work on the farm and other jobs far from home and comeback later tired. No time to sit with their teenagers for any sexuality discussions. Religious leaders should therefore increase their efforts in rendering social welfare services in the Kishika community where they find themselves. Religious leaders can be a link between the community and the government so as to alleviate the hard living condition by creating job opportunities for them near home so that they can find time to parent, communicate and educate their teens.

Church leaders' needs to engage its efforts in increasing sexuality discussions in Bible studies, community seminars on sex matters in order to inform people who might not enter into the Church auditorium for any reason.

Suggestions for Further Research

The sexual education of teenagers is a complex subject that requires many studies and many interventions for it to be understood. A small amount of studies like mine have tried to provide some understanding on sexual education in Kishika, but there is a lot of that that still need to be done. Indeed, further research may be conducted on the contribution of parental sexual education to the teens' sexual behaviour as that is considered to be instrumental in reducing the number of unwanted pregnancies as well as HIV/AIDS and other sexual related issues.

A study of cultural barriers to parental sexual education may be conducted as it has been observed by this researcher that despite the availability of sexual information on radio, television and non-governmental organization orientations, some parents are still ignorant and are bent to hold unto cultural taboos on sex education.

There is also a need for a comparative study of sources of sexual education of teenagers in rural and urban areas.

Conclusion

This study aimed to examine the extent of parental involvement in sex education with teenagers in Kishika community, specifically in the Bassa Local Government area of Plateau state. To that end, the study investigated why some parents were willing, and some unwilling to be involved in sexual education with their teenagers. It also examined the challenges that parents face in their involvement in sex education of teenagers. It then aimed to determine what type of support parents need to be better involved in sex education of their teenagers. The data for this project were collected using oral interview among 50 parents.

This study had been motivated by the fact that parental involvement in sexual education contributes to significant positive knowledge and building of good sexual attitudes among teenagers. Sexual education helps teenagers in gaining a positive view of sexuality, provides them with information and skills about taking care of their sexual health, and helps them make sound decisions regarding their sexuality. The lack of this education may lead teenagers to suffer from many sexual related problems such as STDs, HIV/AIDS, unintended pregnancies and abortion.

Considering on the one hand the fact that many sexual related problems such as STDs, HIV/AIDS and early pregnancies are prevalent in some parts of Nigeria, and on the other hand, the lack of sufficient studies on sexual education in Bassa Local Government area, especially in Kishika, it seemed a window of opportunity to the researcher. Thus, the research focused on the involvement of parents in teenage sexual education. The study assessed different factors that constitute obstacles to the sexuality education involvement of parents with teenagers in Kishika. In fact, the Kishika community culture, lack of adequate education by parents, and lack of time emerged as major obstacles to the sexual education involvement of parents.

The study used literature review and oral interview. Based on the methodology used in the research, the researcher formulated sets of questions directed to respondents that allowed examination on how involved each of them were in their teenager's sexual education.

It is therefore discovered in the study that majority of parents have not stood as sexual education agents to the teenagers in Kishika. The reason is that majority of the parents feel sexuality education is against their culture, the next highest reason is lack of time by parents in Kishika and then others feel they have no enough knowledge to discuss some issues such as HIV/AIDS, STIs and sexual related issues.

However, the biggest barrier to sexuality education in Kishika as identified by the respondents was culture.

APPENDIX

Oral Interview Questions

I am Augustine Uteno Solomon Obaje, a student in the Education Department, Jos ECWA Theological Seminary JETS, and an affiliated Seminary to the University of Jos.I am embarking on the study"Evaluating the State of Parental Involvement on Sex Education: A case study of Kishika Community." The interview is geared towards bringing out the views and experiences of parents in relation to the sexuality education of their teens in Kishika. In order to avoid mentioning of names, I will keep all of your responses and names confidential. Your participation in the course of this interview shall be voluntary. The interview will be conducted in Kishika community, Bassa Local Council Area of Plateau State, Nigeria. The interviews will be recorded using audio recording. Is that okay by you? Do you have any questions before we begin?

Part A

Question 1. How long have you been parents?

Question 2. What is your level of education?

Question 3. What is your occupation?

Question 4. How many teens do you have in your home as a parent?

Part B

Question 5 a. Have you ever discussed sexuality issues with your teens?

b. What sexuality topic(s) have you discussed with your teen?

c. How often do you discuss sexuality topics with your teens?

Question 6. Why is it difficult for you to be involved in sex education with your

teens?

Question 7. Why are you interested in being involved in sex education with your

teens?

Question 8. What are the challenges that you have faced in your efforts to give sex

Education to your teens?

Question 9. What support do you want that would help you carry out sex education

with your te

References

Ajibade, G. O.(2013). Same-Sex relationships in Yoruba culture and
tradition. *DOI*: 10. 1080/900918369.2013.77486

Alaba, O. (2004). Understanding sexuality in the Yoruba culture.

ARSRC 2004 https: //www.semanticscholar.org

Alimi, (2015) a well-known Nigerian gay and gay activitst, "If you say being
gay is not African, you don't know your history"
https://www.theguardian.com/coomentsfree/2015/sep09/being-
gay-african-historyhomosexuality-christainity

Amadiume, I. (1987). *Male daughters, female husbands: Gender and sex in an
African society.*
London: Zed books

Arimoro, A. (2018). "When love is a crime: is the criminalization of same sex
relations in nigeria a protection of Nigerian culture? *Liverpool Law
Review,* 39(2), 221 238

Asare, S. (2014). Erotic expressions in adowa dance of the Asante: The stimulating gestures, costuming and dynamic drumming. *Journal of Music and Dance*, vol 4 (1), pp. 109.

Anyaora, F.O. (2012). Sex Taboos as Regulatory Measure against Sexual Immorality among the
      Igbo People of Anambra state. University of Ibadan: Institute of African Studies, MPhil dissertation.

Caldwell, J.C (1991). The Destabilization of the Traditional Yoruba Sexual
      System. https:www.jstor.org

Clark, G. (1999). Mothering, Work, and Gender in Urban Asante Ideology and Practice. *American Anthropologist*, vol. 101, no 4, pp. 717-729
https://www.jstor.org

Davies, D. (2002). *Anthropology and Theology.* Oxford: Berg.

Damehin, P. A. O. (1993). Sexual Attitudes in Traditional and Modern Yoruba society.
      https://journals.sgaepub.com
Fadipe, N. A. (1970). *The Sociology of the Yoruba.* Ibadan: Ibadan University Press, pp. 301309.
Huber, L. R, and Graybill, R. (2020). *The Bible, Gender, and Sexuality*: Critical
      Readings. Bloomsbury publishing.
Ige, A. S. and Owoyemi, J. O. (2016). Paul Concept of Sexual Activity in
      Marriage: An Exegetical Study of 1 Corinthians 7:1-5 in the African
      Perspective. *Asian Journal of Social Sciences, Arts and Humanities*, vol.
      4, No 4, Pp. 35-45, 2016.

Irinoye, O. O (2005). The conceptions of sexual relationships among the
      Yoruba people in Nigeria. https://researchspace.ukzn.za

Msibi, Thabo. (2011). *"The Lies We Have Been Told: On (Homo) Sexuality in*

Africa."Africa
        Today 58 (1):

Mbiti, J. S. (1992). *Introduction to African Religion.* East African publishers.

Mkasi L. P. (2016). African Same-Sexualities and indigenous knowledge; creating a space for dialogue within patriarchy,*Verbum Ecclesia* vol.137n.2pretoria 2016.

Nyansi, S. 2013. Dismantling reified African culture through localized homosexuality in Uganda. *Cult Health Sex.* 2013:15(8): pp 952-67.

Obaje, A. (2020). Parental Sex Education: Kishika Plateau State Nigeria.Mauritius:LAP LAMBERT Academic Publishers, pp. 1.

Obiero, B. A. (2010). *Sex, Consent and Power: A Case study of Sex-related Cultural Practices among the Luo Community of Kenya.* Dissertation, Master's Degree University of Zimbabwe.

Okafor S O. (2018). The Indigenous Concept of Sexuality in African Tradition and Globalization. *Glob J Reprod Med.*

Oyesanya, F (2020). Ifa practice and perversions of natural order. *Paper presented to Ifa devotees.*

Oyewumi, O..(1997). *The Invention of Women: Making an African Sense of Western Gender Discourses.* Minneapolis: University of Minnesota Press.

Robbins, J. (2006). Anthropology and Theology: An awkward relationship? *Anthropological   Quarterly* 79.2, pp 285-294.

Riggs, T. (2014). *Worldmark Encyclopedia of religious practices.* Gale publishers

Thatcher, A. (Ed.)2014. *The Oxford Handbook of Theology, Sexuality, and Gender.* Oxford University press.

Uram, N. E. (2019). The Values and Usefulness of Same-Sex Marriages among the Females in Igbo Culture in the Continuity of Lineage or Posterity. https://doi.org/10.1177/2158244019850037

Ukpokolo, C. (2010). Gender, space and power in the indigenous Igbo socio-political organization. *Pakistan Journal of Social Sciences*, 7, pp. 177-186.

Woggen, H.A. (1981). A Biblical and Historical Study of Homosexuality. *Journal of Religion and Health,* Vol. 2. No. 2, Springer.

The Code of Canon Law. (1986 Liturgical Publishers.

Akinboye, J.O. *Guidance and Counseling Strategies for Handling Adolescent and Youth Problems*. Ibadan: University Press, 1987.

Balswick, Jack and Balswick, Judith. *The Family: A Christian Perspective on the Contemporary Home.* Grand Rapids, Michigan: Baker Books House, 1992.

Dike, C.C. *Understanding Friendship, Love, Sex.* Enugu: Rabboni Publishers, 2000.

Dobson, James. *Raising Children.* Wheaton, Illinois: Tyndale House Publishers Inc., 1982.

___________. *Preparing for Adolescence.* Wheaton, Illinois: Tyndale House Publishers, 1995.

Fafunwa, Babs A. *History of Education in Nigeria.* Ibadan: NPS Educational Publishers Limited, 2004.

Kore, Danfulani. *Promoting Healthy Marriage and Family Life.* Kaduna: Baraka Press and Publishers Ltd., 2004.

___________. *Culture and the Christian Home.* Jos: ACTS, 2012.

Kunhiyop, Waje S. *African Christian Ethics.* Nairobi: Hippo Books, 2008.

Lar, Telfim. *Sexuality Education for All.* Jos: Akins Press and Services Ltd., 2010.

Mbiti, John. *African Religion and Philosophy.* London: Heinemann Educational
    Publishers, 1989.

McGrath and Congoire. *Africa – Our Way of Love and Marriage.* Ibadan:
    Ambassador Publication, 1983.

Morakinyo, P.O. *Sex Education for Disciplined Youth.* Ibadan: Shallom Publications,
    2002.

Ndirangu, J.M. *Youth in Danger: A Hand Book for Teachers, Students, Parents,
    Pastors and Community Workers.* Nairobi: Uzima Press, 2000.

Robert, Clark. *Christian Education: Foundation for the Future.* Chicago: Moody
    Press, 1991.

Sala, Harold J. *Raising Godly Kids.* Kaduna: Evangel Publishers Ltd., 2001.

Sean, McDowell. *Sexual Purity.* Grand Rapids: Zondervan Publishing House, 2005.

Tim, Clinton and Mark. *Sexuality and Relationship Counselling.* Grand Rapids:
    Barker Books, 2010.

Wardell, B.P. *Boys and Sex.* New York: Delacorte Del, 1991.

Wehmier, Sally. *Oxford Advance Learners Dictionary.* Oxford: Oxford University
    Press, 2006.

White, John. *Parents in Pain.* Leicester: Inter-varsity Christian Fellowship, 1979.

Newspaper

Yunusa, L. Ami. "Teenage Abortion and its Hazards." *Leadership Newspaper* (4
    October 2015): 1.

Journals

Alaba Olugboyeya, "Understanding Sexuality in the Yoruba Culture" *Cultural Research Journal* 5 (2004): 11-22.

Alldered, and Epstein. "Teachers' View of Teaching Sex Education: Pedagogy and Models of Delivery." *Journal of Educational Enquiry* 4/1 (2003): 80 -97.

Darroch J.E. "Changing Emphasis in Sexuality Education Family Planning Perspectives." *Highland Medical Research Journal* 6 (2000): 204-232.

Gibbs, N. "How Should We Teach Our Children about Sex." *Journal of Sex Education*, 3 (1993):60-63.

Lena L. "Sexuality Education in Schools." *South African Journal of sex Education*

52 (2000): 87-92.

Oyenike Alake Oyinloye. "Sexual Education for Wholesome Sexual Behavior Among in-School Nigerian Adolescents." *Sex Education Journal* 41(January 2014): 4-8.

Internet Sources

Adogu, P. "Review of Problems of Adolescent Sexual Behaviour and the Role of Millennium Development Goals." *International Journal of Clinical Medicine*. Cited 26 January 2016. Online: http://www.scirp.org/journal/ijcm http://dx.doi.org/10.4236/ijcm.2014.515126.

Avert. "Abstinence Sex Education and HIV Prevention." No page. Cited 16 February 16 2016. Online: http://www.avert.org/abstinence.htm.

IPPF. (2011) "From Evidence to Action: Advocating for Comprehensive Sexuality Education." No page. Online: March, 2016 fromhttp://www.ippf.org/resource/evidence-action-advocating-comprehensive-sexuality-education.

Michael Sidibe (2009*).* "Youth and Comprehensive Sexuality Education." No page. Cited 16 February 2016. Online: https://www.un.org/development/desa/youth.

Mesce D. and Clifton Donna. "Understanding Social Problems." No page. Cited 16 March 2016. Online: https://books.google.com.ng/books.

The Palo Alto Medical Foundation 2011 *"Teenage Growth and Development: 11-14 Years".*http://www.pamf.org/parenting-teens/health/growth-development/growth.html.

UNESCO, 2009. *International Technical Guidance on Sexual Education* Retrieved February 16, 2016 from http://www.siecus.org/index.cfm?fuseaction.

Unpublished Materials

Adepoju, A. *Sexuality Education in Nigeria: Evolution, Challenges and Prospects.* In African Regional Sexuality Resource Centre. UnderstandingHuman Sexuality. 24th March, 2005.

Akintunde, D.O. and Ayantayo, K. *Sexuality and Spirituality: Possible Bed mates in the Religious Terrain in Contemporary Nigeria.* Department of Religious Studies, University of Ibadan, Lagos Nigeria. June 9, 2005.

Kirby,Douglas. *No Easy Answers on Teen Pregnancy.* Washington: 1997.

Santelli, John. *"Abstinence-only Education Policies and Programs."* A Position paper of the Society for Adolescent Medicine, River State Nigeria, 2006.

Printed by Books on Demand GmbH, Norderstedt / Germany